SQL Weaknesses on Database Processing

Anybody who works with SQL should know its weaknesses

O. F. Domejean

**I dedicate this publication to the
most important persons in my life
my mother who passed away,
my loved wife and daughter.**

CONTENTS

About the Author

Msc. Oswaldo F. Domejean has over 15 years of experience in Database Technology. He got a Master degree in Mathematical Engineering and Informatics in the area of Applied Mathematics. He is currently in charge of a Master Degree Program in Computer System Administration at the "Bolivian Catholic University". He teaches graduate and postgraduate courses in Database and Computer Systems technologies. He is a reviewer and published papers related to the field of research Applied Relational Theory, Temporal Databases and other areas of research in Universities around Latin-America and Spain. He has been student in a specialized course given by Mr. Chris J. Date at University of California – Los Angeles (UCLA). He belongs to the IBM®'s program "Academic Initiative". He was a United Nation (UN) Computer System consultant in a variety of projects.

PREFACE

This book describes some interesting aspects of the weaknesses and conflictive aspects that the language SQL has in Database Processing, it includes some characteristics of the language that are valid from the perspective of the mathematical theory of Logic, but in the queries could lead us to misinterpretations of results.

The intent of this book is to be used along with SQL books because it focuses specifically on the weaknesses and conflictive aspects of the language SQL.

This work is an essential resource for any IT professional who works with SQL databases, because the quality of the information in a SQL database depends entirely on the quality of the database queries, for this reason is essential to know the weaknesses and conflictive aspects of the language SQL to build correct queries. It's assumed that the reader has an intermediate knowledge of the language SQL.

This publication consists of the following seven chapters that describes in detail the aspects of the language related to its weaknesses and conflictive characteristics of it.

1. "Introduction"
This one has a description of some general aspects of the Database field related to the language SQL, and describes in detail the Database that is used in the examples of this publication.

2. "The Interpretation of null"

In this chapter we analyze the *null* mark that SQL has to represent the concept of Missing Information, which can bring us some problems in the interpretation of query result, besides from the fact that there exist some other possibilities of interpretation for this mark in Data Processing.

3. "The Relational Algebra Operations"

In this one you can find an analysis of the lack of equivalency between two possibilities of elaborating queries, one using the Relational Algebra Operations in SQL and the other one using the traditional SQL (i.e. using simple joins).

4. "The conditions EXISTS, IN, ANY and ALL"

In this one we analyze the problems that these conditions show when they have elements that include *null* or the empty set, in such cases the results of the queries can lead us to misinterpretations as it is described in this chapter.

5. "The Aggregation Operators"

This chapter explores the various problems we can have at the time of elaborating queries using the SQL aggregation operators like SUM, AVG, etc., which have a particular behavior when *null* or the empty set are present.

6. "The Implication"

SQL is based on Logic, that's why we can build logical expressions like the Implication that has a series of aspects that we should consider avoiding errors in interpretations of query formulation as it is described in this chapter.

7. "Operations INSERT, UPDATE and DELETE"

In this chapter we analyze some problems that are found with the SQL operations INSERT, UPDATE and DELETE as a consequence of the problems studied in previous chapters of this publication.

This work is based on the ANSI/SQL taking into account the standard elements of SELECT, INSERT, UPDATE and DELETE, this set plus the extensions of SQL with operations from the Relational Algebra are precisely the purpose of this study.

All the examples mentioned in this publication have been verified in the language SQL of the Database Management System DB2® from IBM®, the situation is practically the same and in some cases still worse in other DBMS SQL.

Acknowledgments

I want to thank to my family and to some colleagues and friends who helped me with their opinions and suggestions. I am also very grateful with Mr. Chris J. Date, he has always been very kind to me in answering some questions related to the Relational Theory.

1

1. INTRODUCTION

The Database Management Systems, in general, are based on the Relational Model, theory that has been defined by E. F. Codd over thirty years ago and it continues to be one of the most stable theoretic foundations in Data Processing. These systems use SQL which is considered to be the most used language to retrieve information from Databases.

This work is an analysis of some interesting aspects of the weaknesses of SQL in Databases, but not all the aspects analyzed in these chapters are related to the SQL's weaknesses, there are some other aspects that are valid from the perspective of the mathematical theory of Logic but in the queries could lead us to misinterpretations of results.

This work is based on the ANSI/SQL taking into account the standard elements of SELECT, INSERT, UPDATE and DELETE, this set plus the extensions of SQL with operations from the Relational Algebra are precisely the purpose of this study.

All the examples mentioned in this work have been verified in the language SQL of the Database Management System DB2®, the situation is practically the same and in some cases still worse in other DBMS SQL.

In order to describe the weaknesses and other characteristics of SQL we have an example Database named "Debit Cards" described below. You will notice that in the chapters some Relation Variable[1] tuples vary from the data of the example Database, this was done for improving issues in the illustration of the analyzed aspects.

The Example Database

The example database named "Debit Cards" is referred to withdrawals and deposits of funds using Debit Cards. In the case of withdrawals of funds there are three options, ATMs (Automatic Teller Machine) withdrawal, funds transfers between accounts and purchases of products or services (see the example database below).

Description of Relation Variables

Most of the Relation Variables are self-explained, except for DEPOSIT and WITHDRAWAL; in these cases we

---

[1] Traditionally named Relation of the Relational Model

have the following semantic considerations:

Deposits of Funds:

- The customers deposit funds both in his accounts and in some other's accounts in DEPOSIT.
- In a deposit of funds it is inserted the related withdrawal code in DEPOSIT (see the point following)
- Customers who deposit funds not necessarily have Bank's accounts.
- The deposits cannot be done by using ATMs.

Withdrawals of Funds:

There are three types of withdrawals of funds, ATM's withdrawals of funds, transference of funds between accounts and purchase of products or services.

ATM's withdrawal of funds:
- An ATM's withdrawal of funds is inserted with ATM's code from where the withdrawal was accomplished; the withdrawal cannot exceed the total of deposits of the related account.

Funds transfer:
- In a fund transfer we have a withdrawal of funds from one account and a deposit of funds toward another account for which the amount should be the same.
- In a fund transfer, the withdrawal code, from where the funds came, is inserted in the DEPOSIT.
- The account's owner of the withdrawal of funds should be the same as the customer who deposits the funds.

- In funds transfer there is not exist the ATM's code.

Products or services purchase:
- The products or services purchase is inserted as a withdrawal of funds; in this case the associated ATM code does not exist.

Database: "Debit Card"

CUSTOMER

CUST	NAME	CITY
1	Perez	Madrid
2	Smith	New York
3	Bonner	Paris
4	Chen	Hong Kong

ACCOUNT

ACC	CUST	BNK
8123	2	BB
4551	2	BA
3212	3	BC
3529	3	BC
4254	1	BB
4572	1	BA

BANK

BNK	BANK
BA	Bank A
BB	Bank B
BC	Bank C

ATM

ATM	CITY	BNK
a1	Paris	BA
a2	Roma	BB
a3	Madrid	BA
a4	Rio	BB
a5	Paris	BC

DEPOSIT

DEP	ACC	DATE	CUST	AMOUNT	WIT
d1	8123	12/05/2005	2	2000	*null*
d2	4551	17/05/2005	1	3000	*null*
d3	4254	21/05/2005	1	2500	*null*
d4	3212	25/05/2005	1	400	r2
d5	3529	27/05/2005	4	1500	*null*
d6	3212	12/06/2005	2	450	r5
d7	4254	15/06/2005	3	150	r7

WITHDRAWAL

WIT	ACC	DATE	AMOUNT	ATM
r1	8123	25/05/2005	300	a1
r2	4254	25/05/2005	400	*null*
r3	4551	05/06/2005	300	*null*
r4	3529	10/06/2005	250	a2
r5	8123	12/06/2005	450	*null*
r6	4254	12/06/2005	200	*null*
r7	3529	15/06/2005	150	*null*
r8	3212	17/06/2005	200	a3
r9	4551	20/06/2005	500	a4

Note..- Primary keys are in bold

2

2. THE INTERPRETATION OF *null*

Introduction

In DBMS SQL there is a need to insert the fact that at any given moment we do not have a value for an attribute, in such case the DBMS SQL gives us the possibility of using *null* to represent the concept of Missing Information which can bring us some problems in query results, as it will be shown in this chapter. Beyond Missing Information there exist some other possibilities of interpretation for the *null* mark in Data Processing which can also lead us to confusion at the time of interpreting query results in a Database.

null in SQL

E. F. Codd in [2] presented *null* as a mean to represent Missing Information (i.e. the absence of information at a given moment), and later in [3] he made a classification of it in two types. The first type corresponds to Missing and Applicable Information, that is, the *null* we know from SQL, which allows us to represent the lack of information at a given moment.

The second type corresponds to Missing and Inapplicable Information which does not have a correspondent in SQL; therefore we have to struggle with this type of information. In reality, as is examined further on, *null* is not enough to represent these types of information; and I think this situation limits SQL from giving us a more complete answer in query formulations.

In the standard SQL besides from *null* the symbol *unknown* has been defined [5] to represent a third logical value. Then, we would have another possibility in the result of a logical expression, not only *TRUE* or *FALSE* but also *unknown*. But SQL uses *null* to represent both Missing Information and that mentioned third truth value. The problem is that this language represents two concepts with just one symbol *null*, and of course it doesn't differentiate them in query results.

Then, as the example below shows, when we have an expression that has one or more variables with *null* (e.g. Missing Information), it is reasonable to think that the result is unknown, because this is precisely what happens, it is not known the result, that is why the result should be that third logical value *unknown*.

20

Considering the variables X and Y as numerical, when at least one of these variables has *null*, this expression should give us a result of *unknown*.

$$X < Y$$

But, in this case SQL presents us *null* as a result, if we negate the expression, in the same way with at least one of the variables with *null*, the result is also *null*, not *unknown* as we could expect. What happen is that in SQL we never have that third truth value *unknown* as a result.

There is another problem with *null*, in the operation of equality one *null* is not equal to other *null*, it makes sense, but for example in the case of the SQL Intersect operation from the Relational Algebra, the things changes because a *null* is equal to other *null*, as it is shown in the following example:

AA

A	B
a_1	*null*
null	b_1

AB

A	B
a_1	*null*

```
SELECT X.A, X.B
FROM AA X
INTERSECT
SELECT Y.A, Y.B
FROM AB Y
```

A	B
a_1	*null*

Note the fact that in the result of the intersection the tuples (a_1, *null*) of AA and AB, are considered equal, if the result is interpreted from the perspective of symbols it is correct, but in this case there is a particular semantics, that is, the concept of Missing Information for this case represented by *null*, or maybe some other interpretation in the context of a database. The point is that we do not know if the tuples are or aren't equal, this fact can lead us to misinterpret the result.

If SQL is used to accomplish the intersection operation, that is, the join of AA and AB on the base of the comparison of all these table's attributes, we don't obtain the same answer in the case of the example it generates the empty set, these aspects will be analyzed in a chapter later in this publication.

Some meanings of *null*

In Databases you not only require a mean to represent the fact that some information in a given moment is missing, represented by *null*, but there can also exist other meanings [6] of *null* depending on the semantics of a Relation Variable in a Database. An example that illustrates this fact is the following:

WITHDRAWAL

WIT	ACC	DATE	AMOUNT	ATM
r1	8123	25/05/2005	300	a1
r2	4254	25/05/2005	400	*null*
r3	4551	05/06/2005	300	*null*
r4	3529	10/06/2005	250	a2

In this Relation Variable we can have three types of withdrawal of funds; the first one is when really the withdrawal is associated to an ATM, in the example the value a1 for the withdrawal r1.

The second possibility shows up when a customer purchases a product or service, the payment of the service or product is inserted by means of a withdrawal, in the example the code of withdrawal r3 with *null* in the attribute ATM because it is not associated to an ATM.

The third possibility shows up when a customer makes a transference of funds, a process that has two steps, first is the withdrawal of funds, in the example the code of withdrawal r2, and second is the correspondent deposit with code d4 in the Relation Variable DEPOSIT (see the example Database), for this case also *null* is stored in the attribute ATM.

Definitively we cannot regard the second and third possibility as Missing Information because they are not, but we can consider them, for example, Inapplicable Information, precisely what it means in this context because there isn't not exist an ATM value for transference of funds or a purchase.

Now, in the case of an ATM's withdrawal of funds, you can find the case, for any reason, that there isn't an ATM code from where the withdrawal of funds has been accomplished, in the example the value r4 from ATM instead of having a2 could have *null*, this case corresponds to Missing Information, so that the ambiguity is amplified.

As you can see we have at least two different meanings of *null* for a withdrawal of funds, first Missing Information and second Inapplicable Information and maybe others, these concepts represented by the same *null,* which definitively can carry us confusion in the interpretation of answers to queries using SQL.

The following is an example that illustrates the possibility of a misinterpretation in the result of a database query.

"Get the accounts and the total amount of deposits that are greater than 1000 for the Bank with code BB"

ACCOUNT

ACC	CUST	BNK
8123	2	BB
4551	2	BA
4254	1	null

DEPOSIT

DEP	ACC	...	AMOUNT	...
d1	8123		2000	
d2	4551		3000	
d3	4254		2500	
d7	4254		150	

```
SELECT B.ACC, SUM(B.AMOUNT) AS TOTAL
FROM ACCOUNT A, DEPOSIT B
WHERE A.ACC = B.ACC
      AND A.BNK = 'BB'
GROUP BY B.ACC
HAVING SUM(B.AMOUNT) > 1000
```

The query gives the tuple (8123, 2000). Taking the following as a first case, the account number 8123 has an amount greater than 1000, the same happens with the account 4254 that has a total amount of 2650, but in this case it is not known the Bank which it belongs to, because of *null* in the attribute BNK, for that reason we do not have the account 4254 in the result.

Taking the following as a second case, what happens with the Relation Variable ACCOUNT if it has the attribute value BC for BNK in the account 4254. In this case the condition gives *FALSE* therefore we do not obtain this account in the result.

The problem is that we obtain only one answer, I mean no tuples for the account 4254 in two different situations, in the first case with *null* in the attribute BNK, the answer can be interpreted like this:

> "It is not known if there exist some client
> accounts that have the total amount of
> deposits greater than 1000 in the Bank BB"

On the other hand, in the second case we have BC for the attribute BNK then we have:

> "There is not an account that has the
> total amount of deposits greater than
> 1000 in the Bank BB"

In summing up, these are two interpretations and just one answer. SQL does not differentiate *null* in a correct way; therefore we should be careful with the interpretation given to answers of this language when *null* is present.

The use of special values

The alternative to the utilization of *null* is the use of special values [7], which can represent various meanings found in attributes. This alternative has a significant advantage, the use of two valued logic with only *TRUE* and *FALSE*.

The problem is that any value that we choose as special may cause us trouble because DBMS SQL doesn't differentiate the chosen special value with other common values.

In the case of the examples examined above if we use the especial value 'XYZ', which represent Missing Information, the result would be the same, that is, one answer with two different interpretations.

In order to illustrate the problems in choosing a special value, we added an attribute named INCREMENT to the Relation Variable DEPOSIT in which an increment in terms of percentage is calculated depending on the amount of the deposit that clients have. However, not everyone will have an increment; we choose zero as the special value in this case. The following example illustrates this point:

"Get the accounts and the increased amount of deposits for all customers"

DEPOSIT

DEP	ACC	...	AMOUNT	INCREMENT
d3	4254		2500	0.2
d5	3529		1500	0

```
SELECT ACC, (AMOUNT * INCREMENT) AS TOTAL
FROM DEPOSIT
```

The result is:

ACC	TOTAL
4254	50
3529	0

As we see in the case of the account '4254' we have the correct calculation, but with the account '3529' we obviously get as a final result of zero. We could have used *null* instead of zero, but the result is similar, the account '3529' with an empty TOTAL. Therefore we can misinterpret the result.

I think that in SQL we should have a way to differentiate the concepts of Missing Information, Inapplicable Information, and other interpretations that might exist for an attribute value in a database. The problem is that SQL just has one symbol, the *null* mark, to represent only the concept of Missing Information, but there may be other interpretations that can occur in attributes of a database. Then, I think that the query results from an SQL database should be divided into the following possibilities:

- The attribute values that fulfill the conditions of the query.
- The empty set when none of the conditions are fulfilled.
- If it happens, the information that some attribute values meets the different interpretations as "Unknown", "Inapplicable", etc., in the database.

This division would give us all the information we should receive from any SQL query to a database.

Conclusion

We have seen in this chapter that the third truth value *unknown* that we can find in the standard SQL is never used when the result of a query is precisely unknown. The use of *null* in the language SQL could bring us some problems related to equality and Relational Algebra Operations in query interpretation. Another aspect is that not only the lack of information is necessary to insert in an attribute, but also exists some other possibilities that definitively may cause us a misinterpretation in Data Processing. The utilization of the special values decreases the problems because we are still in a two valued logic, but it could also lead us to confusion in query results. The point is that we have to be conscious and be careful with SQL when the aspects analyzed are present.

References and Bibliography

[1] E. F. Codd: "A Relational Model of Data for Large Shared Data Banks". *CACM 13, No. 6 (June 1970)*

[2] E. F. Codd: "Extending the Database Relational Model to Capture More Meaning". *ACM. Transactions On Database Systems 4*, No. 4 (December 1979)

[3] E. F. Codd: "Missing Information (Aplicable and Inaplicable) in Relational Databases", *ACM SIGMOD Record 15*, No 4 (December 1986).

[4] E. F. Codd: "More Commentary on Missing Information in Relational Databases (Applicable and Inapplicable Information)". *ACM SIGMOD Record 16, No 1* (March 1987).

[5] C. J. Date, H. Darwen: "Basic Language Elements". *A Guide to SQL Standard (4th Edition)*. Addison-Wesley 2000.

[6] C. J. Date: "NOT Is Not 'Not'". *Relational Databases Writings 1985 – 1989*. Addison Wesley, 1990.

[7] C. J. Date: "Missing Information". *An Introduction to Database Systems(8th Edition)*. Addison –Wesley (2004).

[8] International Business Machines Corporation (IBM®): "DB2 SQL Reference, Volume 1 and 2". *DB2 for Linux, UNIX and windows manuals*. http://www.ibm.com/

[9] A. Warden: "ADVENTURES IN RELATIONLAND: Into The Unknown". *Relational Databases Writings 1985 – 1989.* Addison Wesley, 1990.

3

3. THE RELATIONAL ALGEBRA OPERATIONS

Introduction

In general, in the DBMS SQL we have the possibility of elaborating queries with some of the Relational Algebra operations [3]; among them we find the union, intersection and others. Then, there are two possibilities of elaborating queries, one using the mentioned operations and the other one using the traditional SQL (i.e. using simple joins). We find some problems in the equivalency in these two alternatives of elaborating queries when *null* is present, in these cases the answers are different in equivalent queries.

The Relational Algebra operations

The problems analyzed in this chapter come from the fact that SQL consider one *null* equal to other *null* for the Relational Algebra operations in SQL, but in the case of equality operation one *null* is different to other *null*. It is a very strange perspective but this is the way SQL works.

Taking two projections of the Relation Variable ACCOUNT, considering only the attributes CUST and BNK, for issues of the example both Relation Variables do not have Primary Keys and in this case we interpret *null* as Missing Information:

RA

CUST	BNK
1	BB
2	null
null	BA
null	null
3	BC

RB

CUST	BNK
3	BC
null	BA
2	null
null	null

Union operation

In this case the only possibility that we have to the union of two Relation Variables is the use of the SQL's UNION operation. We do not have other alternative in the traditional SQL. The example using the Relation Variables RA and RB is the following:

```
SELECT CUST, BNK FROM RA
UNION
SELECT CUST, BNK FROM RB
```

The result is:

CUST	BNK
null	BA
1	BB
3	BC
2	null
null	null

The union operation gives us a result consisting of all the tuples whether they have *null* or not, and it eliminates duplicates, but SQL consider the tuple (2, null) in both Relation Variables as if they were duplicates, that is not necessarily correct since *null* can have different values in both tuples, something similar happens with the tuple (null, null). The result of the query should be *unknown* in these cases because this is what it really is.

Intersect operation

In this case there are two possibilities for formulating queries in a database. One is using the SQL's INTERSECT operation, and the other is using the traditional SQL. An example of the first possibility is the following:

```
SELECT CUST, BNK FROM RA
INTERSECT
SELECT CUST, BNK FROM RB
```

The result is:

CUST	BNK
null	BA
3	BC
2	null
null	null

As is observed the INTERSECT operation consider the tuples (2, null) in both Relation Variables as if they were duplicates, this is not necessarily correct because *null* can correspond to different values, something similar happens with some other tuples.

In the case of the second possibility, the INTERSECT operation can be stated as a join of both Relation Variables RA and RB including in the condition all the common attributes. The two mentioned possibilities can be stated in an equivalent way, so we would expect to obtain the same result for both queries, but there is not such equivalency. An example of the second possibility is the following:

```
SELECT RA.CUST, RB.BNK
FROM RA, RB
WHERE RA.CUST = RB.CUST
AND RA.BNK = RB.BNK
```

The result is:

CUST	BNK
3	BC

In this case observe the fact that in the conditions SQL consider one *null* different to other *null*, that is why it doesn't include tuples with *null*, this result is completely different from the one that we obtained using the operation INTERSECT.

Considering that *null* in the Relation Variables means Missing Information, there is another problem in the result, we do not get the fact that there are some tuple values that the database does not "know", precisely the tuples with *null*, and this is also information that we should receive as a response, and then the answer is not complete.

As we can see there isn't exists an equivalency between the operation INTERSECT and the correspondent join operation using conditions in the traditional SQL.

Difference operation

In this case there are also two possibilities of formulating queries in a database. One is using the SQL's EXCEPT operation, and the other is using the condition EXISTS from the traditional SQL. An example of the first possibility is hereby illustrated:

```
SELECT CUST, BNK FROM RA
EXCEPT
SELECT CUST, BNK FROM RB
```

The result is:

CUST	BNK
1	BB

The same as in the case of INTERSECT, observe that the EXCEPT operation consider the tuple (2, *null*) in both Relation Variables as duplicates, this is not necessarily correct because *null* can correspond to different values, something similar happens with the other tuples.

In this case we do not get the fact that there are some tuple values that the database does not "know", precisely the tuples with *null*, and this is also information that we should receive as a response, then the answer is not complete.

In the case of the second possibility we have that the EXCEPT operation can be stated using the condition EXISTS from traditional SQL. The two mentioned possibilities can be stated in an equivalent way then we would obtain the same result for both queries, but there is not such equivalency. An example of the second possibility is the following:

```
SELECT CUST, BNK
FROM RA
WHERE NOT EXISTS (SELECT * FROM RB
            WHERE RB.CUST = RA.CUST
            AND RB.BNK = RA.BNK)
```

The result is:

CUST	BNK
1	BB
2	*null*
null	BA
null	*null*

This result is completely different from the one that we obtained using the operation EXCEPT. The tuple (1, 'BB') does not have any problem since it only exists in RA, although in the case of the tuple (2, *null*), this exists in both RA and in RB; something similar happens with the other RA's tuples.

The result of the query makes sense taking into account that it considers the tuple (2, *null*) of both Relation Variables different, which is correct because we do not know the values of *null* at that point. What happen is that we obtain this result because of the particular behavior that EXISTS has when it deals with *null* (detailed description in the chapter "The Condition EXISTS, IN, ANY and ALL" in this publication).

Cartesian Product Operation

This operation of the Relational Algebra can be stated as a join without conditions in the traditional SQL; however the result is not very practical in terms of information. In order to describe this operation we have included the following Relation Variable:

RC

CITY
Madrid
New York

```
SELECT * FROM RA, RC
```

The result is:

CUST	BNK	CITY
1	BB	Madrid
2	*null*	Madrid
null	BA	Madrid
null	*null*	Madrid
3	BC	Madrid
1	BB	New York
2	null	New York
null	BA	New York
null	*null*	New York
3	BC	New York

This result is the combination of all possible attribute values between both Relation Variables, now it is pertinent to mention that because of the fact that there are no conditions that filter the result, we do not have problems with the *null*.

Restrict operation

This operation of the Relational Algebra in SQL is done by stating some conditions with the attributes of a Relation Variable, let's examine this:

```
SELECT RA.CUST
FROM RA
WHERE RA.BNK = 'BB'
```

In this case the most relevant consideration is that this query offers us a non empty result just for the tuples that fulfill the condition; it doesn't consider in the result the ones with *null* which in this case means unknown.

Project operation

This operation of the Relational Algebra in SQL is conducted by specifying the attributes that we require in the result, like in the case:

```
SELECT CUST FROM RA
```

In this case we have the client codes of the Relation Variable RA including duplicates if it has, in the case of *null* the query give us all of them that appears in the attribute. It is important to mention that this characteristic does not agree with the definition of the project operation of the Relational Algebra [3], which says that it does not give us duplicate tuples in the result. To avoid the duplicates we can use the operator DISTINCT from SQL.

Join operation

This operation of the Relational Algebra can be expressed with the traditional SQL by specifying the conditions that we required in the operation, for example in the case:

```
SELECT A.CUST, B.BANK
FROM RA A, RB B
WHERE A.BNK = B.BNK
```

The result of this operation depends on the values of the attributes that are evaluated in the condition WHERE, in the event that some of these values of attributes had *null*, the correspondent tuple does not appear in the result.

Division operation

This operation of the traditional SQL does not have a Relational Algebra counterpart, for this reason the division in the SQL can be stated on the base of the following equivalency [2]:

```
FORALL V (p(V)) ≡ NOT (EXISTS V (NOT p(V)))

FORALL: Universal quantifier
EXISTS: Existential quantifier
V: Variable
p(V): Truth valued function
```

That is, the Universal Quantifier can be expressed with two negations using the Existential Quantifier; an example of this is the following:

"Get customer's codes that have accounts in all the Banks"

RG

CUST	BNK
1	BA
1	BB
1	BC
2	BB
2	BC
2	BD
3	BA
3	BB
1	null

RH

BNK
BA
BB
BC
null

```
SELECT DISTINCT X.CUST
  FROM RG X
  WHERE NOT EXISTS (SELECT *
        FROM RH Y
        WHERE NOT EXISTS (SELECT *
              FROM RG
              WHERE RG.BNK = Y.BNK
              AND RG.CUST = X.CUST))
```

The result of this query is the empty set, since in RG and in RH we have the tuples (1, *null*) and (*null*) respectively. We can interpret the answer as if there isn't exist customers that are associated to all the Banks in RH, but this is not correct, the answer should be *unknown* because we do not know if *null* of RH and RG corresponds or not to the same information, for that reason we can misinterpret the answer.

There exist several possibilities in the answer of this query depending on the inclusion of *null* in tuples, that is, in the event that both RG and RH does not have the tuples (1, *null*) and (*null*) respectively, the result of the query corresponds to customer's code 1, this is correct because the customer with code 1 is associated with all of the Banks of the Relation Variable RH.

In the case that we have the tuple (1, BD) in RG and in RH the tuple (*null*), the result of the query does not generate any tuple, in this case we can interpret as if there does not exist a customer associated to all the Banks in RH, but again this is not correct for the fact that, in reality, this information should be *unknown* because of *null*.

Equivalency of Intersection with double Difference

The Intersect operation can be expressed in equivalent form like a double difference [3] of the Relation Variables implicated, that is:

```
A INTERSECT B
```

is equivalent to:

```
A MINUS (A MINUS B)
B MINUS (B MINUS A)
```

Let's examine this equivalency using the Relational Algebra in SQL with the example Relation Variables as follows:

```
SELECT CUST, BNK FROM RA
INTERSECT
SELECT CUST, BNK FROM RB
```

The result is:

CUST	BNK
null	BA
3	BC
2	null
null	null

In order to interpret this result we should consider the observations mentioned in the Intersect operation in this chapter.

The analysis begins using the SQL difference operation EXCEPT, for which first we make the difference of the Relation Variables, according to the equivalency above, and a view VA is created.

```
CREATE VIEW VA AS
SELECT CUST, BNK FROM RA
EXCEPT
SELECT CUST, BNK FROM RB
```

The result is:

CUST	BNK
1	BB

Next we accomplished the correspondent difference between RA and the view VA:

```
SELECT CUST, BNK FROM RA
EXCEPT
SELECT CUST, BNK FROM VA
```

This operation gives the same result as using the INTERSECT operation. It is also verified the following operation:

B MINUS (B MINUS A)

Using the traditional SQL, for this same case we have the following operation:

```
SELECT CUST, BNK
FROM RA
WHERE NOT EXISTS (SELECT * FROM RB
                  WHERE RB.CUST = RA.CUST
                  AND RB.BNK = RA.BNK)
```

The result is:

CUST	BNK
1	BB
2	*null*
null	BA
null	*null*

With this operation we create a view VA, then:

```
SELECT CUST, BNK
FROM RA
WHERE NOT EXISTS (SELECT * FROM VA
      WHERE VA.CUST = RA.CUST
      AND VA.BNK = RA.BNK)
```

This operation generates the same result as the Intersect operation INTERSECT using the double minus mentioned previously. In most cases we cannot find an equivalency between Relational Algebra Operations and traditional SQL, but in some cases like this one there is such equivalency. In the case of the answer with the traditional SQL what we get is due to the particular behavior of the condition EXISTS when *null* is present (detailed description in the chapter "The Condition EXISTS, IN, ANY and ALL" in this publication).

Conclusion

The points examined in this chapter really show us that there are not such equivalencies between the traditional SQL and the SQL using Relational Algebra Operations, these problems happen because of the processing of *null* from the SQL perspective. The point is that in reality we should be conscious of these aspects and choose the adequate alternative, either using the traditional SQL or the SQL using Relational Algebra operations for a query.

References and Bibliography

[1] E. F. Codd: "Extending the Database Relational Model to Capture More Meaning". *ACM. Transactions On Database Systems 4*, No. 4 (December 1979)

[2] C. J. Date: "A Little Bit of Logic". *Database in Depth: Relational Theory for Practitioners*. O'Reilly Media. 2005.

[3] C. J. Date: "Relational Algebra". *An Introduction to Database Systems(8th Edition)*. Addison –Wesley (2004).

[4] R. Elmasri, S. B. Navathe: "The Relational Database". *Fundamentals of Database Systems (3th Edition)*. Pearson. 2002.

[5] International Business Machines Corporation (IBM®): "DB2 SQL Reference, Volume 1 and 2". *DB2 for Linux, UNIX and windows manuals*. http://www.ibm.com/

4

4. THE CONDITIONS
EXISTS, IN, ANY AND ALL

Introduction

In SQL there exist an equivalency between the conditions EXISTS, IN, ANY and ALL to the effect that the first three have a similarity with the Existential Quantifier, and the last one with the Universal Quantifier. The problem shows up when these conditions have elements that include *null* or the empty set, in such cases the result of the queries can lead us to misinterpretations as it is described in this chapter.

The set of possible values for the Quantifiers

There exists a difference in the kind of possible elements that can have the condition EXISTS and the conditions IN, ANY and ALL. In the case of the condition EXISTS the possible elements of an expression are tuples in relations, in this case represented with t_i, and then the possible values are:

```
(t₁, t₂, ..., tₙ)
(Φ)
(t₁, t₂, ..., null, ..., tₙ)
(null)
```

With Φ the empty set.

On the other hand, in the cases of the conditions IN, ANY and ALL the possible elements of an expression are attribute values, in this case represented with elements e_i, then the possible values are:

```
(e₁, e₂, ..., eₙ)
(Φ)
(e₁, e₂, ..., null, ..., eₙ)
(null)
```

With Φ the empty set.

Case analysis with the conditions EXISTS, IN, ANY and ALL

There exist some difficulties with the conditions EXISTS, IN, ANY and ALL in the equivalency between them when *null* or the empty set are present. The descriptions of these problems are explained in five cases.

It will not be taken into account the following two cases, an expression with the condition EXISTS that have tuples $(t_1, t_2, \ldots, t_n)$, this condition gives a result *TRUE*, because it evaluates the existence of tuples. Something similar happens in the case of the conditions IN, ANY and ALL, when these ones have the elements $(e_1, e_2, \ldots, e_n)$, the result of the expression will be *TRUE, FALSE* or *null* depending on the result of the logical expression.

Case N° 1.- Conditions NOT IN (*null*), NOT (ANY (*null*)) and NOT EXISTS (Φ)

C. J. Date showed in [3] that the conditions IN and EXISTS don't behave in an equivalent way when they have *null* or the empty set in an expression that use these conditions. Besides from the lack of equivalency and the problems with the various possibilities in interpretation the *null* mark can have, I think, it's a very important issue that SQL doesn't take into account in query results those concepts of Missing Information, Inapplicable Information, and other interpretations that might exist for an attribute value in a database, because it is also information that SQL should give us.

I think that in SQL we should have a way to differentiate the concepts of Missing Information, Inapplicable Information, and other interpretations that might exist for an attribute value in a database. The problem is that SQL just has one symbol, the *null* mark, to represent only the concept of Missing Information, but there may be other interpretations that can occur in attributes of a database. As we said in Chapter 2 the query results from an SQL database should be divided into the following possibilities:

- The attribute values that fulfill the conditions of the query.
- The empty set when none of the conditions are fulfilled.
- If it happens, the information that some attribute values meets the different interpretations as "Unknown", "Inapplicable", etc., in the database.

This division would give us all the information we should receive from any SQL query to a database. Let's analyze with an example the problems in query results and interpretation that could happen in a database.

The following example includes the case of the condition ANY for the equivalency it has with the condition IN and EXISTS. The example is:

"Get ATM's cities and bank codes which doesn't have withdrawals that are less than 300"

ATM

ATM	CITY	BNK
a1	Paris	BA
a2	Rome	BB
a3	Madrid	BA

WITHDRAWAL

WIT	...	AMOUNT	ATM
r1		300	a1
r2		400	*null*
r6		200	*null*
r9		500	a4

Let's recall the semantics the Relation Variable WITHDRAWAL has. In this Relation Variable we can have three types of withdrawal of funds; the first one is when really the withdrawal is associated to an ATM, in the example the value a1 for the withdrawal r1.

48

The second possibility shows up when a customer purchases a product or service, the payment of the service or product is inserted by means of a withdrawal, in the example the code of withdrawal r6 with *null* in the attribute ATM because it is not associated to an ATM.

The third possibility shows up when a customer makes a transference of funds, a process that has two steps, first is the withdrawal of funds, in the example the code of withdrawal r2, and second is the correspondent deposit with code d4 in the Relation Variable DEPOSIT (see the example Database), for this case also *null* is stored in the attribute ATM because it's not associated to an ATM.

Definitively we cannot regard the second and third possibility as Missing Information because they are not, but we can consider them, for example, Inapplicable Information, precisely what it means in this context because there isn't not exist an ATM value for transference of funds or a purchase.

Now, in the case of an ATM's withdrawal of funds, you can find the case, for any reason, that there isn't an ATM code from where the withdrawal of funds has been accomplished, in the example the value r9 from ATM instead of having a4 could have *null*, this case corresponds to Missing Information, so that the ambiguity is amplified. Let's see the following queries:

```
SELECT A.CITY, A.BNK
FROM ATM A
WHERE A.ATM NOT IN (SELECT B.ATM
                    FROM WITHDRAWAL B
                    WHERE B.AMOUNT < 300)
```

```
SELECT A.CITY, A.BNK
FROM ATM A
WHERE NOT (A.ATM = ANY (SELECT B.ATM
                        FROM WITHDRAWAL B
                        WHERE B.AMOUNT < 300))
```

The result of these two queries is the empty set, now examining in more detail we see that the result of the sub-queries is *null* in both cases, therefore we are in the cases NOT IN (*null*) and NOT (ANY(*null*)). Remember that in this and the next example, *null* doesn't represent Missing Information but Inapplicable Information.

```
SELECT A.CITY, A.BNK
FROM ATM A
WHERE NOT EXISTS (SELECT *
                FROM WITHDRAWAL B
                WHERE B.AMOUNT < 300
                AND A.ATM = B.ATM)
```

The result of this query is a list with all Cities and Bank codes of the Relation Variable ATM, now examining in more detail, in this case we see that the result of the sub-query is the empty set, then we are in the case of EXISTS (Φ), and we know that in the Relational context if the condition EXISTS has the empty set as a result, then the expression is *FALSE*, and with the Boolean operator NOT in the expression we obtain *TRUE*, therefore we get all Cities and Bank codes.

So far in this case three equivalent alternatives has been given in the solution of the query with two different results, in the first two we had the empty set as a result, on the other hand, in the latter case we got a list with all the Cities and Bank codes, in the three cases I think the answer for the tuples with *null* should have been Inapplicable Information, because this is also information, and very important although, that SQL should give us. This is a very relevant problem which can lead us to misinterpret the result.

It is also important to consider that the behavior of the conditions IN and ANY when they are not negated, that is in the cases IN (*null*) and ANY (*null*) in the sub-queries, give us also *null* as a result, besides from the problems in interpretation we have analyzed.

Case N° 2.- Conditions NOT IN (Φ), NOT (ANY (Φ)) and NOT EXISTS (Φ)

When we have the empty set as the only element of the conditions IN, ANY and EXISTS, the behavior of these three is equivalent, since in these cases we obtain *FALSE* as a result, we noticed that this behavior is the same as in the Existential Quantifier. We use the following example to illustrate this fact using a non-existent city.

"Get the Bank names which does not have ATMs in London"

BANK

BNK	BANK
BA	Bank A
BB	Bank B
BC	Bank C

ATM

ATM	CITY	BNK
a1	Paris	BA
a2	Rome	BB
a3	Madrid	*null*
a4	*null*	BB
a5	Paris	BC

```
SELECT A.BANK
FROM BANK A
WHERE A.BNK NOT IN (SELECT B.BNK
            FROM ATM B
            WHERE B.CITY = 'London')
```

```
SELECT A.BANK
FROM BANK A
WHERE NOT (A.BNK = ANY (SELECT B.BNK
            FROM ATM B
            WHERE B.CITY = 'London'))

SELECT A.BANK
FROM BANK A
WHERE NOT EXISTS (SELECT *
            FROM ATM B
            WHERE B.CITY = 'London'
            AND A.BNK = B.BNK)
```

The answer is a list of all Banks of the Relation Variable BANK, therefore the equivalency is verified.

Case N° 3.- Condition EXISTS (*null*)

In this case we have *null* as the only element of the condition EXISTS, this condition is equivalent to the behavior of the Existential Quantifier in the sense that it verifies the existence of at least one tuple, if this condition is fulfilled it gives *TRUE* otherwise *FALSE*, the problem is that the tuples can contain *null* [2], which can bring us some problems as is illustrated in the example following:

"Get customers codes from the Bank 'BB' who made ATM withdrawals greater than 300"

ACCOUNT

ACC	CUST	BNK
8123	2	BB
3212	3	BC

WITHDRAWAL

WIT	ACC	. . .	AMOUNT	ATM
r1	8123		300	a1
r5	8123		450	*null*
r8	3212		200	a3

```
SELECT A.CUST
FROM ACCOUNT A
WHERE A.BNK = 'BB'
AND EXISTS (SELECT B.ATM
            FROM WITHDRAWAL B
            WHERE A.ACC = B.ACC
            AND B.AMOUNT > 300)
```

The result of the query is the customer code '2' that belongs to account 8123, if the ATM's *null* would mean that the correspondent ATM was not inserted at the time of the transaction, that is, value unknown, the answer would be correct. The problem is that in the case of this attribute the meaning of *null* is not only Missing Information but also the purchase of products or services or a funds transfer between accounts, therefore the answer can confuse us.

Now, the result of the sub-query contains just one tuple, for which the attribute ATM has *null*, that is, this attribute is not empty, this result is very interesting because the condition EXISTS identifies the existence of "something" in this case *null* for which simply generate *TRUE* without taking into account that in this case *null* represent a Transference of Funds.

I think, it's a very important issue that SQL doesn't take into account the meaning of *null* in the query result of the example, that's why in this case the answer doesn't make sense because of the interpretation that *null* has in this query, and this is also information that SQL should give us.

It is important to mention that we have selected B.ATM in the sub-query and not "*" as is usually used, but even with asterisk the answer is the same. Therefore we should take care with the interpretation that we give to answers of queries with the condition EXISTS when there are tuples with *null*.

Case N° 4.- Condition IN or ANY with $(e_1, e_2, ..., null, ..., e_n)$

In this case we have the conditions IN and ANY with the set $(e_1, e_2, . . ., null, . . ., e_n)$, in this set we have an element *null* that in this case represents Missing Information. The problem is that if we do not have an attribute value that fulfils the condition in the set, the result of the two conditions IN and ANY is *FALSE*, but it should be *unknown* because of *null*. The following example illustrates such fact using the condition IN, in the case of using ANY the situation is the same.

"Get customer's names from Hong Kong who made deposits greater than 400"

CUSTOMER

CUST	NAME	CITY
1	Pérez	Madrid
2	Smith	New York
4	Chen	Hong Kong

DEPOSIT

DEP	ACC	. . .	CUST	AMOUNT	. . .
d4	3212		1	400	
d5	3529		null	1500	
d6	3212		2	450	

```
SELECT NAME
FROM CUSTOMER
WHERE CITY = 'Hong Kong'
AND CUST IN (SELECT CUST
             FROM DEPOSIT
             WHERE AMOUNT > 400)
```

The result of this query is the empty set. The only tuple that would possibly be able to fulfill the condition in the sub-query is the deposit d5 since the amount is greater than 400. The sub-query generates as a result the list $(null, 2)$, in this case *null* correspond to Missing Information, and therefore the customer with code 4 is a possible candidate, which is why the answer should be *unknown* instead of the empty set.

Case Nº 5.- Condition `ALL` with (e_1, e_2, ..., `null`, ..., e_n) and `ALL` (Φ)

There are two aspects of the condition `ALL` that may lead us to some problems in interpretation of results. In the case of the first aspect, in the condition `ALL` when *null* is one of the elements of the `ALL'`s set (e_1, e_2, ..., `null`, ..., e_n), generate *FALSE*, in this case *null* is considered as Missing Information, this result is not correct since we really do not know the precise answer because of the presence of *null*, the correct answer should be *unknown*.

In the case of the second aspect, we have the empty set as the only element of the condition `ALL`, its behavior is equivalent to the Universal Quantifier in the Relational context in which gives us *TRUE* when the set is empty, this is a result that may lead us to misinterpretations in SQL queries using this condition as we examine below.

An example of a problem with the first aspect mentioned above is as follows:

"Get the accounts in which the deposits are greater than all the deposits present in the Bank's accounts `BC`"

ACCOUNT

ACC	CUST	BNK
8123	2	BB
4551	2	BA
3212	3	BC
3529	3	BC
4572	1	BA

DEPOSIT

DEP	ACC	...	AMOUNT	...
d1	8123		2000	
d2	4551		3000	
d3	4254		2500	
d4	3212		400	
d5	3529		null	
d6	3212		450	

```
SELECT A.ACC
FROM DEPOSIT A
WHERE A.AMOUNT > ALL (SELECT B.AMOUNT
                      FROM DEPOSIT B, ACCOUNT C
                      WHERE C.ACC = B.ACC
                      AND C.BNK = 'BC')
```

The result of this query is the empty set, in this case we can interpret *null* of deposit d5 as Missing Information. The result of the sub-query generates the set (400, *null*, 450), for which there isn't exist a deposit that is greater than all the elements of this set, therefore the sub-query generates *FALSE*.

The result obtained is not precise for the fact that one of the elements is *null*, therefore we really do not know such fact. The correct answer should be *unknown* and not the empty set that lead us to the interpretation that there isn't exist accounts that have amounts of deposit greater than all the deposits present in the Bank's accounts 'BC'.

As it was mentioned above in the second aspect when the set associated to the condition ALL is the empty set, the result of the sub-query is *TRUE*. In order to illustrate this fact we use a variant of the previous query in the following example:

```
SELECT A.ACC
FROM DEPOSIT A
WHERE A.AMOUNT > ALL (SELECT B.AMOUNT
                      FROM DEPOSIT B, ACCOUNT C
                      WHERE C.ACC = B.ACC
                      AND C.BNK = 'XY')
```

Here, we see in the Relation Variable ACCOUNT that the Bank's code 'XY' does not exist, then the result of the sub-query is the empty set, and as we identified above when this happens the behavior of the condition ALL is equivalent to the Universal Quantifier in the Relational context, it generates *TRUE*, so that we obtain all the DEPOSIT's accounts, then the answer can cause a misinterpretation of the result since the Bank's code 'XY' does not exist.

The sub-query associated to the condition ALL can even be an absurd statement, while the result of the sub-query expression were empty it will always be *TRUE*. This is not an error from the perspective of Logic, it is a consequence related to the definition of the condition ALL. Then, we have to be conscious that this situation may let us fall down in interpretation errors.

Conclusion

The conditions EXISTS, IN and ANY represent somehow the Existential Quantification of Logic, we have seen that some problems can show up when *null* or the empty set are present, because of this there isn't exists a complete equivalency between the SQL's perspective and the Logic. In the case of the condition ALL we have to be careful because in some cases, like the studied in this chapter, the behavior of the condition is correct from the perspective of Logic, however it can cause us confusion in answers of queries to Databases. Definitively, it is very important to be conscious of the behavior of these conditions when *null* or the empty set is present to avoid misinterpretations.

References and Bibliography

[1] C. J. Date: "A Little Bit of Logic". *Database in Depth: Relational Theory for Practitioners*. O'Reilly Media. 2005.

[2] C. J. Date: "EXISTS Is Not 'Exists'". *Relational Databases Writings 1985 – 1989*. Addison Wesley, 1990.

[3] C. J. Date: "Oh No Not Nulls Again". *Relational Databases Writings 1989 – 1991*. Addison Wesley, 1992.

[4] C. J. Date: "Relational Calculus". *An Introduction to Database Systems(8th Edition)*. Addison –Wesley (2004).

[5] R. Elmasri, S. B. Navathe: "The Relational Database". *Fundamentals of Database Systems (3th Edition)*. Pearson. 2002.

[6] W. K. Grassman, J. P. Tremblay: "Predicate Calculus". *Logic and Discrete Mathematics*. Prentice Hall, 1997.

[7] International Business Machines Corporation (IBM®): "DB2 SQL Reference, Volume 1 and 2". *DB2 for Linux, UNIX and windows manuals*. http://www.ibm.com/

[9] A. Warden: "ADVENTURES IN RELATIONLAND: Table_Dee and Table_Dum". *Relational Databases Writings 1985 – 1989*. Addison Wesley, 1990.

5

5. THE AGGREGATION OPERATORS

Introduction

SQL has aggregation operators for numerical operations, these operators have a particular behavior when *null* or the empty set is present, and these can lead us to query misinterpretations. This chapter explores the various problems we can have at the time of elaborating queries to Databases when we use these operators, which definitively affect the accuracy that is required and should exist when numerical values are processed.

The Aggregation Operators

In order to illustrate some of the problems the SQL's Aggregation Operators sum, average, etc. have, we use the following set:

$$X = x_1, x_2, \ldots, x_n$$

We regard as the smallest value x_1 and the biggest value x_n, then the Aggregation Operators are:

```
(a)  Sum: SUM (X) = x₁ + x₂ + ... + xₙ
(b)  Maximum Value: MAX (X) = xₙ
(c)  Minimun Value: MIN (X) = x₁
(d)  Average: AVG (X) = (x₁ + x₂ + ... + xₙ)/n
(e)  Count: COUNT (X) = n
```

We are going to consider the following two cases of possible values that the set X can have:

1. The presence of one or more *null* in the set X
2. The empty set in X

It is important to notice that in the case that set X is empty, the operators (a), (b), (c) and (d) give us *null* as a result, on the other hand, in the case of (e) the result is zero.

The operator SUM ( )

With this operator we analyze the case when *null* is present in the mentioned set X, the following example illustrates the SQL behavior:

"Get the total withdrawals for each customer's account"

WITHDRAWAL

WIT	ACC	...	AMOUNT	...
r1	8123		300	
r4	3529		250	
r5	8123		450	
r6	4254		null	
r7	3529		null	

```
SELECT ACC, SUM(AMOUNT) AS TOTAL
FROM WITHDRAWAL
GROUP BY ACC
```

The result is:

ACC	AMOUNT
8123	750
3529	250
4254	null

This result presents some of aspects for analysis, in the case of the tuple with account code 3529, we see that it has a withdrawal of 250 and *null* (in this case interpreted as Missing Information), the result of the query is 250, then SQL is not taking into account *null* as an element, so that the correct result for this account should be *unknown*.

And what happens if we add in the condition that the total amount of withdrawal is less than 800, and then the query is:

```
SELECT ACC, SUM(AMOUNT) AS TOTAL
FROM WITHDRAWAL
GROUP BY ACC
HAVING SUM(AMOUNT) < 800
```

The result is:

ACC	AMOUNT
8123	750
3529	250

The result of this query gives us all the accounts, except the account 4254 that disappeared from the result. What happens is that, in the first example, we did not have a condition to fulfill, but in this second example we have the condition HAVING which is not fulfilled because of *null*, and this is the reason why the account 4254 is not in the result of the query.

In the case that the operator SUM (set) has the empty set as the only element, the result is *null* and not zero as it would be expected. The following example illustrates such fact:

"Get the deposit codes for customers that have a total of withdrawals less that 300"

```
SELECT DISTINCT A.DEP
FROM DEPOSIT A
WHERE (SELECT SUM (B.AMOUNT)
          FROM WITHDRAWAL B
          WHERE A.ACC = B.ACC) < 300
```

DEPOSIT

DEP	ACC	...
d2	4551	
d3	4254	
d5	3529	
d7	4254	

WITHDRAWAL

WIT	ACC	...	AMOUNT	...
r2	4254		100	
r4	3529		250	
r6	4254		50	
r7	3529		150	

The result is:

DEP
d3

We observe in the example data that the deposit of the account 4551 corresponding to the deposit code d2 does not have any withdrawal of funds in WITHDRAWAL, for this reason the operator SUM of the sub-query has the empty set as its only element, and the answer for this operator is *null*. This is the reason why the deposit related to the account 4551 is not included in the answer of this query. Later it's going to be analyzed what happen when this operator is compared with the operator COUNT.

The operator AVG ( )

The operator average AVG also has problems when *null* is present in the mentioned set X. The example following:

"Get the average of withdrawals for each customer's account"

WITHDRAWAL

WIT	ACC	. . .	AMOUNT	. . .
r1	8123		300	
r2	4254		400	
r5	8123		450	
r6	4254		*null*	
r9	4551		500	
r10	4254		100	

```
SELECT ACC, AVG (AMOUNT) AS AVERAGE
FROM WITHDRAWAL
GROUP BY ACC
```

The results is:

ACC	AVERAGE
8123	375
4254	250
4551	500

In the result we observe that the average for the case of the account `4254` has been calculated on the base of values (`400, null, 100`) and the result that we obtain is `250`, that is, (`400 + 100`)`/2`, therefore the operator of average `AVG` has not taken into account *null* as an unknown element, then the correct answer should be *unknown*.

In the same way as in the case of the operator `SUM`, when `AVG (set)` has the empty set as the only element, the result of the query is *null,* this is not correct because the result should be an error specifically because of the operation of average.

The Operators MAX ( ) and MIN ( )

We are going to use the operator `MAX ( )`, the analysis for the operator `MIN ( )` is applicable in equivalent form. We are going to use the set X when *null* is present to illustrate this operator's behavior, let's use the example table of the previous point:

"Get the maximum values for each withdrawal account"

```
SELECT ACC, MAX(AMOUNT) AS MAXIMUM
FROM WITHDRAWAL
GROUP BY ACC
```

The result is:

ACC	MAXIMUM
8123	450
4254	400
4551	500

It should be noticed that the account with code `4254` has three values (`400,   null,   100`), in this case we regard *null* as Missing Information; the query result is `400`, it is not considering the fact that *null* may correspond to a larger value than `400,` therefore the correct answer should be *unknown*.

The operator COUNT ( )

The operator `COUNT   (set)   ` has a particular behavior when we have the element *null* in the set X above mentioned, considering that we have the set with *n* elements and one of them is *null*, the result of `COUNT   (X)` is *n-1*, because this operator does not consider *null* as an element of the set. On the other hand in the event that we use the symbol asterisk instead of the name of attribute like in the operator `COUNT   (*),` the result is *n* since in this case the operator considers all the elements of the set without taking into account the values of X. An example that illustrates this fact is the following:

R

CITY
Paris
Rome
Madrid
null
London

```
SELECT COUNT (CITY)
FROM R
```

The result is four because we just have four cities different from *null*, however, if we use COUNT (*) instead of COUNT (CITY) in the query, the result is the value of five.

The operator COUNT ( ) vs. SUM ( )

As we have said above when the operator COUNT (set) has the empty set as its only value, the result is zero, on the other hand in the cases of SUM, AVG, MIN and MAX with the same conditions the result is *null*. An example that illustrates a situation in which the answer can lead us to misinterpretation, is the following:

"Get the accounts and the total deposits greater than 1500, for customers that has a total withdrawals less than 300"

```
SELECT DISTINCT A.ACC, SUM(A.AMOUNT) AS DEPOSITS
FROM DEPOSIT A
WHERE (SELECT SUM (B.AMOUNT)
            FROM WITHDRAWAL B
            WHERE A.ACC = B.ACC) < 300
GROUP BY A.ACC
HAVING SUM (A.AMOUNT) > 1500
```

DEPOSIT

DEP	ACC	...	AMOUNT	...
d2	4551		3000	
d3	4254		2500	
d5	3529		1500	
d7	4254		150	

WITHDRAWAL

WIT	ACC	...	AMOUNT	...
r2	4254		100	
r4	3529		250	
r6	4254		50	
r7	3529		150	

The result is:

ACC	DEPOSITS
4254	2650

We observe in the data that the deposit of the account 4551 does not have any related withdrawal, that is, it does not exists in the Relation Variable WITHDRAWAL, in such sense the operator SUM of the sub-query has the empty set as the only element, for this reason the mentioned account is not included in the result.

Now taking this result into account, we want to get the accounts and the total deposits that have a number of withdrawals less than three, in such case we change the operator SUM by COUNT in the sub-query and also the condition is changed to withdrawals less than three, then we have:

```
SELECT DISTINCT A.ACC, SUM(A.AMOUNT) AS DEPOSITS
FROM DEPOSIT A
WHERE (SELECT COUNT (B.AMOUNT)
            FROM WITHDRAWAL B
            WHERE A.ACC = B.ACC) < 3
GROUP BY A.ACC
HAVING SUM (A.AMOUNT) > 1500
```

The result is:

ACC	DEPOSITS
4254	2650
4551	3000

In this result we find the account 4551 that exists only in Relation Variable DEPOSIT, this happens for the fact that the operator COUNT in the sub-query has the empty set for this account, therefore this operator has generated the value zero, which permits that the mentioned account appears in the result.

Comparing this result with the previous one, we see that there is not exists an equivalency when we have the empty set as the only element for the operators SUM and COUNT, in such sense we can misinterpret the answer.

Conclusion

In this chapter we have examined that data processing associated to numerical calculations does not work properly when we have *null* or the empty set. Another aspect that we saw is the lack of symmetry in terms of results between the operators SUM, MIN, MAX and AVG, and the operator COUNT when we have the empty set. Definitively the analyzed operators do not behave as we would expect in the mentioned cases, we get answers that affect the exactness that we required, and should exist at the time of processing numerical values, and again we should be conscious about these problems to avoid misinterpretations of query results.

References and Bibliography

[1] T. M. Connolly, C. E. Begg: "SQL: Data Manipulation". *Database Systems – A practical approach to design, implementation and management (4th Edition)*. PEARSON Education S.A., 2005.

[2] R. Elmasri, S. B. Navathe: "The Relational Database". *Fundamentals of Database Systems (3th Edition)*. Pearson. 2002.

[3] International Business Machines Corporation (IBM®): "DB2 SQL Reference, Volume 1 and 2". *DB2 for Linux, UNIX and windows manuals.* http://www.ibm.com/

6

6. THE IMPLICATION

Introduction

SQL is based on Relational Calculus, which in turn is based on Logic, in such sense; we can build logical expressions like, in this case, the Implication. In Logic the Implication has a series of aspects that we should consider to avoid errors in interpretations of query formulation. This chapter describes some conflictive aspects that are correct from the perspective of Logic, but from the perspective of SQL, can cause problems.

The Implication in SQL

Some SQL queries can be formulated using the Implication, for which we should understand some inherent aspects of this theory. In order to illustrate these aspects we use the concepts antecedent represented by P and consequent represented by Q. There are three logically equivalent alternatives of the Implication:

$$P \Rightarrow Q \equiv \; \sim P \; OR \; Q \equiv \; IF \; P \; THEN \; Q$$

For the analysis, we have the following Truth Table of this operation:

IMPLICATION's TRUTH TABLE

No	P	Q	~P	Q	~P OR Q
1	T	T	F	T	T
2	T	F	F	F	F
3	F	T	T	T	T
4	F	F	T	F	T

T: TRUE, F: FALSE

In this Truth Table we observe some particular aspects. In the case of number one and two; when the antecedent is *TRUE* the result of the expression is the same as the consequent. In the case of number three, we see that we are departing from a false premise in the antecedent and the whole expression is *TRUE*. In the case of number four, the situation is worse, since we are departing from both a false antecedent and consequent and we obtain *TRUE* in the whole expression. In spite of this conflictive aspect, the mentioned expressions are considered valid in Logic.

We have the following examples of queries in order to illustrate these aspects of the Implication:

"Get customers codes that if they have money transfers from ATM a3, the Bank of the customer account has the code BA".

This query departs from a false premise because there should not exist a fund transfer associated with an ATM, because of one of the integrity rules from the example database. In the case of the condition related to the Bank of the customer account, there is no problem, it can be *TRUE*. This query can be formulated from the Implication perspective like this:

```
IF fund transfer has ATM's code a3
THEN the customer account belongs to the Bank BA
```

The query can be expressed in an equivalent way using one of the expression mentioned above ~P OR Q like this:

```
NOT   (DEPOSIT.WIT = WITHDRAWAL.WIT
       AND WITHDRAWAL.ATM = 'a3')
OR
       (ACCOUNT.ACC = WITHDRAWAL.ACC
       AND ACCOUNT.BNK = 'BA')
```

As we see the antecedent:

```
(DEPOSIT.WIT = WITHDRAWAL.WIT
AND WITHDRAWAL.ATM = 'a3')
```

is *FALSE* as we said above, on the other hand the consequent:

```
(ACCOUNT.ACC = WITHDRAWAL.ACC
AND ACCOUNT.BNK = 'BA')
```

is *TRUE* (in this query we consider so). We are in the case of line number three in the truth table above, and then we get the result *TRUE*, considering the case that we have departed from a false antecedent. This logical expression in SQL corresponds to:

```
SELECT DISTINCT C.CUST
FROM DEPOSIT A, WITHDRAWAL B, ACCOUNT C
WHERE NOT (A.WIT = B.WIT AND B.ATM = 'a3')
      OR (C.ACC = B.ACC AND C.BNK = 'BA')
```

ACCOUNT

ACC	CUST	BNK
8123	2	BB
4551	2	BA
3212	3	BC
3529	3	BC
4254	1	BB
4572	1	BA

DEPOSIT

DEP	ACC	...	CUST	AMOUNT	WIT
d1	8123		2	2000	null
d2	4551		1	3000	null
d3	4254		1	2500	null
d4	3212		1	400	r2
d5	3529		4	1500	null
d6	3212		2	450	r5
d7	4254		3	150	r7

WITHDRAWAL

WIT	ACC	...	AMOUNT	ATM
r1	8123		300	a1
r2	4254		400	null
r3	4551		300	null
r4	3529		250	a2
r5	8123		450	null
r6	4254		200	null
r7	3529		150	null
r8	3212		200	a3
r9	4551		500	a4

The result is:

CUST
1
2
3

The result of the query is the three customer codes that we have in the Relation Variable ACCOUNT. The most relevant interpretation that we might be able to give to this answer is that it might be valid to accomplish funds transfers by means of an ATM, which is completely erroneous in the context of the example database. The result is correct from the perspective of Logic, but we have to be conscious of it to avoid misinterpretations of query results.

The other case is with the line number four of the mentioned Truth Table, in this case we have a still worse situation, since both the antecedent and the consequent are false. The following example illustrates such a case:

"Get customers codes that if they have money transfers from ATM a3, the amounts are different"

This query departs from two false premises, the first corresponds to transferences from ATMs (it has been explained in the previous exercise the falseness of this point) and the second one in which the transfer amounts are different, the latter is also false in the context of the example database, since fund transfer is associated with a withdrawal and a deposit with the same amount.

Likewise in the previous example, this query can be expressed from the implication perspective in the following way:

```
IF funds transfer has ATM's code 'a3'
THEN the associated amounts are different
```

The query can be expressed in an equivalent way using the expression above ~P OR Q like this:

```
NOT
        (DEPOSIT.WIT = WITHDRAWAL.WIT
        AND WITHDRAWAL.ATM = 'a3')
OR

        (WITHDRAWAL.ACC = ACCOUNT.ACC
        AND DEPOSIT.AMOUNT <> WITHDRAWAL.AMOUNT)
```

We see that the antecedent is false as we said above, and the consequent is also false, the total result of this expression is *TRUE*. This logical expression in the SQL corresponds to:

```
SELECT DISTINCT C.CUST
FROM DEPOSIT A, WITHDRAWAL B, ACCOUNT C
WHERE NOT (A.WIT = B.WIT AND B.ATM = 'a3')
        OR (B.ACC = C.ACC AND A.AMOUNT <> B.AMOUNT)
```

The result that we obtain is exactly the same as that in the previous case, that is, the three customer codes. In the case of the antecedent the interpretation has been described in the previous exercise, in the case of the consequent the situation is also obvious, since because of a semantic restriction of the example database, there are not different amounts in a fund transfer.

This is a valid case from the perspective of Logic, it is not an error in SQL, and then we have to be conscious of it to be careful in query constructions, otherwise we can misinterpret the answers.

Conclusion

The analysis accomplished in this chapter illustrates several risky aspects in query constructions in SQL when we use logical expressions like in this case the Implication. As we have examined, this is neither a problem of Implication in Logic, nor a problem in SQL. But, we have to be conscious of such conflictive aspects to avoid misinterpretation of answers that we obtain from a database query.

References and Bibliography

[1] C. J. Date: "A Little Bit of Logic". *Database in Depth: Relational Theory for Practitioners*. O'Reilly Media. 2005.

[2] R. Elmasri, S. B. Navathe: "The Relational Database". *Fundamentals of Database Systems (3th Edition)*. Pearson. 2002.

[3] W. K. Grassman, J. P. Tremblay: "Propositional Calculus". *Logic and Discrete Mathematics*. Prentice Hall, 1997.

[4] International Business Machines Corporation (IBM®): "DB2 SQL Reference, Volume 1 and 2". *DB2 for Linux, UNIX and windows manuals*. http://www.ibm.com/

7

7. OPERATIONS INSERT, UPDATE AND DELETE

Introduction

These Operations work with Table Expressions using SQL's SELECT, and also with Conditional Expressions (i.e. Comparison, BETWEEN, IN, etc.). In the previous chapters we examined a series of SQL weaknesses in database processing. In this chapter we analyze some problems that are found with the operations INSERT, UPDATE and DELETE as a consequence of the problems studied in previous chapters of this publication. In this case we find a mayor problem since it is not only related to difficulties in query results, but also to erroneous data in databases.

Operations INSERT, UPDATE and DELETE

In general, with these operations we have two kinds of expressions [3, 4] Table and Conditional Expressions that allow us to make the analysis.

The INSERT operation puts data into databases in two forms, inserts individual tuples and using Table Expressions, the later one interests us in this analysis, for which it's used the SELECT operation. In the cases of the operations UPDATE and DELETE, we will use Conditional Expressions.

We are going to analyze these operations making some references to the SQL weaknesses mentioned in the previous chapters for the fact that we use the same kind of expressions. It is important to notice that in this case the problem is much more serious since we are talking about operations that change values in Relation Variables, these changes can result in erroneous data in databases.

The operation INSERT

The general syntax of the operation INSERT [2] is:

```
INSERT INTO table [(columns)] source
```

In the component "source" of this expression, we are mainly interested on the Table Expression associated with SELECT operation, then we have a plenty range of possibilities for this type of expression.

In order to illustrate some of the problems we have with an insertion operation, we included a couple of tables named `TEMP1` and `TEMP2`, considering that these tables are associated to a migration of data toward the example database, then we have the following insertion:

"Insert in the Relation Variable `ATM` the ATMs such that the associated Bank is not in the city `Montevideo`"

TEMP1

ATM	CITY	BNK
a6	Quito	BB
a7	Vienna	BA

TEMP2

CITY	BNK
Rome	BB
Montevideo	*null*

```
INSERT INTO ATM (ATM, CITY, BNK)
      (SELECT A.ATM, A.CITY, A.BNK
      FROM TEMP1
      WHERE A.BNK NOT IN (SELECT B.BNK
            FROM TEMP2 B
            WHERE B.CITY = 'Montevideo'))
```

The result of this expression does not insert any tuple in the Relation Variable `ATM` and generate a message which mentions that no tuple is found to insert in that Relation Variable `ATM`. What happens is that the nested sub-query in the `SELECT` expression gives us *null* as a result, therefore the total `SELECT` operation give us the empty set, as we saw in the chapter "The condition `EXISTS, IN, ANY` and `ALL`" in this publication, then no tuple is inserted in the Relation Variable `ATM`. The following is an equivalent expression of insertion for the previous one:

```
INSERT INTO ATM (ATM, CITY, BNK)
     (SELECT A.ATM, A.CITY, A.BNK
     FROM TEMP1 A
     WHERE NOT EXISTS (SELECT *
          FROM TEMP2 B
          WHERE A.BNK = B.BNK
          AND B.CITY = 'Montevideo'))
```

In this case the result is different because this query inserts the tuples from TEMP1 into the Relation Variable ATM.

Here we have two equivalent queries that generate different results, what happens is that in this last case the sub-query generates the empty set as a result, therefore the condition EXISTS generates *FALSE* and with NOT both tuples are inserted.

As we saw in the example, in a process of database migration the result of an INSERT can insert or not the tuples depending on how we state the query, therefore there is a possibility to have a database with erroneous information if we are not careful with *null*.

The operation UPDATE

The general syntax of the operation UPDATE [2] is:

```
UPDATE table
SET columns-assignment
[WHERE search-condition]
```

In the case of columns assignment we have the possibility that by means of Table Expressions i.e. using SELECT, a value were assigned to the target Relation Variable, with the restriction that the result of this expression should generate just one value, because it's an individual assignment for the Relation Variable being updated, this possibility will not be taken into account with a concrete example, because we consider that the examples in this and previous chapters in this publication are enough to understand the possible problems of interpretation that can show up in this case.

In the case of the search-condition that corresponds to Conditional Expressions mentioned above, definitely we are interested in this one that can have the following possible conditions:

- Comparison
- BETWEEN
- LIKE
- IN
- ALL - ANY
- EXISTS

As it's seen we practically have all the possibilities in the SQL's conditions. We have this following example to illustrate the problems encountered at the time of updating attribute values in a Relation Variable:

"Increase in 2,5% to individual amounts of deposits, for which the deposited amount is greater than all the amounts of the customer with code 8123"

DEPOSIT

DEP	ACC	. . .	AMOUNT	. . .
d1	8123		2000	
d2	4551		3000	
d3	4254		2500	
d4	3212		400	
d5	3529		1500	
d8	8123		2200	

```
UPDATE DEPOSIT
SET AMOUNT = AMOUNT * 1,025
WHERE AMOUNT > ALL (SELECT A.AMOUNT
      FROM DEPOSIT A
      WHERE A.ACC = 8123)
```

The amounts that we have for the account 8123 are 2000 and 2200, this is the result that we obtain from the sub-query, then the only tuples that fulfill the condition are d2 and d3, which get an increment of 2,5% in their amounts, until this point we do not have any problems. Now what happens if we use a non-existent account like 1111 in the condition of the sub-query in the example:

```
UPDATE DEPOSIT
SET AMOUNT = AMOUNT * 1,025
WHERE AMOUNT > ALL (SELECT A.AMOUNT
                FROM DEPOSIT A
                WHERE A.ACC = 1111)
```

The result of this query is a 2,5% of increment for all the accounts. In this case the sub-query generates the empty set as a result for the fact that there isn't exists the account 1111. As we have seen in previous chapters, when the condition ALL has the empty set as its only element then the result of the condition is *TRUE*. That is why in the results we have a 2,5% of increment for all the amounts of the Relation Variable DEPOSIT.

This is a severe problem, just for the fact that we make a mistake putting a non-existent account (i.e. 1111), the change takes effect for all the amounts of DEPOSIT. This is an aspect that could generate an inconsistent database.

It has to be taken into account that this isn't an error from the perspective of Logic, is a consequence due to the definition of the condition ALL that also isn't erroneous as we saw in previous chapters.

The operation DELETE

The general syntax of the operation DELETE [2] is:

```
DELETE
FROM table
[WHERE Search-Condition]
```

In this case the search-conditions, which correspond to Conditional Expressions mentioned above, have the same operators like Comparison, BETWEEN, LIKE, etc. In order to illustrate the problems with tuple elimination we have the following example:

"Delete the withdrawal of funds that are less than the average of withdrawals that belongs to customer 3529"

WITHDRAWAL

WIT	ACC	...	AMOUNT
r2	4254		400
r4	3529		200
r6	4254		200
r7	3529		*null*
r8	3212		200
r10	3212		100

```
DELETE FROM WITHDRAWAL
WHERE AMOUNT < (SELECT AVG(AMOUNT)
        FROM WITHDRAWAL
        WHERE ACC = 3529)
```

In this Relation Variable we observe that the customer with account `3529` has two elements, `200` and *null*, and the result of the sub-query is the value `200`, which is an error because, as we have seen in previous chapters, the result should be *unknown* since we do not know the value that *null* would have. What happen is that SQL simply does not include *null* in the calculation.

In this case the only tuple that fulfils such condition is `r10` which is eliminated; of course, this elimination is not correct since an erroneous average has been calculated, then we have another possible problem in having erroneous data in a database.

Conclusion

We made an analysis of just some of the consequences that can show up with the operation `INSERT, UPDATE` and `DELETE`, when we are changing data. This happens because of the problems that we found in previous chapters in this publication. The major issue is the fact that in this case the problem is capital since there is a possibility of having erroneous data in a Database.

References and Bibliography

[1] T. M. Connolly, C. E. Begg: "SQL: Data Manipulation". *Database Systems – A practical approach to design implementation and management (4th Edition)*. PEARSON Education S.A., 2005.

[2] C. J. Date, H. Darwen: "Data Manipulation: Noncursor Operations". *A Guide to SQL Standard (4th Edition)*. Addison-Wesley, 2000.

[3] C. J. Date, H. Darwen: "Table Expressions". *A Guide to SQL Standard (4th Edition)*. Addison-Wesley, 2000.

[4] C. J. Date, H. Darwen: "Conditional Expressions". *A Guide to SQL Standard (4th Edition)*. Addison-Wesley, 2000.

[5] R. Elmasri, S. B. Navathe: "The Relational Database". *Fundamentals of Database Systems (3th Edition)*. Pearson. 2002.

[6] International Business Machines Corporation (IBM®): "DB2 SQL Reference, Volume 1 and 2". *DB2 for Linux, UNIX and windows manuals*. http://www.ibm.com/

Index

M

MAX, 60, 64, 66, 68
MIN, 60, 64, 66, 68
MINUS, 41, 42
Missing Information, x, 19, 20, 22, 23, 26, 28, 34, 49, 53, 54, 55, 56, 61, 65

O

operator **AVG**, 63

P

Project, 38

Q

query, x, 19, 24, 27, 33, 36, 38, 40, 41, 44, 50, 53, 54, 56, 57, 59, 61, 62, 63, 64, 65, 66, 67, 68, 71, 73, 74, 75, 76, 79, 81, 82, 84, 86

R

Relation Variable, 14, 22, 23, 24, 26, 32, 37, 38, 40, 48, 49, 50, 52, 57, 67, 74, 81, 82, 83, 84, 86
Relational Algebra, x, xi, 14, 21, 31, 32, 37, 38, 39, 41, 43, 44
Relational Model, 13, 14, 28, 44

S

SELECT, xi, 14, 24, 26, 32, 33, 34, 35, 36, 37, 38, 39, 40, 41, 42, 43, 51, 52, 53, 54, 56, 57, 61, 62, 63, 64, 66, 67, 74, 76, 79, 80, 81, 82, 84, 85
semantic considerations, 15
SQL, 1, i, ix, x, xi, 13, 14, 19, 20, 21, 22, 23, 25, 27, 28, 31, 32, 33, 34, 35, 36, 37, 38, 39, 41, 42, 43, 44, 45, 55, 57, 58, 59, 60, 61, 68, 69, 71, 72, 74, 76, 77, 79, 80, 83, 86, 87
SUM, x, 24, 60, 61, 62, 63, 64, 66, 67, 68

T

traditional SQL, x, 31, 32, 33, 35, 43, 44
Truth valued function, 39

U

union, 31, 32, 33
UNION, 32
Universal quantifier, 39
unknown, 20, 21, 27, 33, 38, 40, 41, 51, 53, 54, 55, 56, 61, 64, 65, 86
UPDATE, xi, 14, 79, 80, 82, 84, 86

W

weaknesses, 1, i, ix, 13, 14, 79, 80